AMAZING BIRDS

By Brenda Williams

Gareth Stevens
Publishing

Please visit our web site at www.garethstevens.com.
For a free catalog describing our list of high-quality books, call 1-800-542-2595 (USA)
or 1-800-387-3178 (Canada). Our fax: 1-877-542-2596

Library of Congress Cataloging-in-Publication Data
Williams, Brenda, 1946–
    Amazing birds / Brenda Williams.
      p. cm. — (Amazing life cycles)
    Includes index.
    ISBN-13: 978-0-8368-8894-2 (lib. bdg.)
    ISBN-10: 0-8368-8894-4 (lib. bdg.)
    1. Birds—Juvenile literature. 2. Birds—Life cycles—Juvenile
literature. I. Title.
    QL676.2.W55   2008
    598—dc22   2007043755

This North American edition first published in 2008 by
Gareth Stevens Publishing
A Weekly Reader® Company
1 Reader's Digest Road
Pleasantville, NY 10570-7000 USA

This U.S. edition copyright © 2008 by Gareth Stevens, Inc. Original edition copyright © 2007 by ticktock Media Ltd.
First published in Great Britain in 2007 by ticktock Media Ltd., Unit 2, Orchard Business Centre, North Farm Road,
Tunbridge Wells, Kent, TN2 3XF United Kingdom

ticktock Project Editor: Ruth Owen
ticktock Project Designer: Sara Greasley
With thanks to: Trudi Webb, Sally Morgan, and Elizabeth Wiggans

Gareth Stevens Senior Editor: Brian Fitzgerald
Gareth Stevens Creative Director: Lisa Donovan
Gareth Stevens Graphic Designer: Alex Davis
With thanks to: Mark Sachner

Photo credits (t = top; b = bottom; c = center; l = left; r = right):
Corbis: 7tl, 7r, 10c, 20tl, 22c. FLPA: 6tl, 8tl, 9 main, 9tl, 15cl, 17t, 17r, 21b, 24b, 25t, 25b, 29cl, 30b. Jupiter images: 14b.
Nature Picture Library: 26, 27. Shutterstock: cover, title page, contents page, 4tl, 4–5 main, 4b, 5t, 7bl, 8c, 8b, 9tr, 10tl,
10br, 11t, 11b, 12tl, 12c, 12b, 13, 14tl, 14–15c, 14cr, 14cl, 15tl, 15tr, 15cr, 15b, 16tl, 16, 18 all, 19, 22tl, 22–23 main, 23tl, 24tl,
28, 29r, 30tl, 31 all. Superstock: 5b, 20 main, 21t. ticktock image archive: map page 6, globe page 22.

Every effort has been made to trace copyright holders, and we apologize in advance for any omissions. We would be
pleased to insert the appropriate acknowledgments in any subsequent edition of this publication.

Printed in the United States of America

1 2 3 4 5 6 7 8 9 10 09 08 07

Contents

Words in the glossary appear in **bold type** the first time they are used in the text.

What Is a Bird?

Ducks and other water birds have waterproof feathers.

Birds have something that no other animals have—feathers! Other animals have wings, and other animals lay eggs, but no other animals have feathers.

Flying birds have stiff feathers that help them fly. They have small, soft feathers called down to help keep them warm.

Beak

Tail

Millions of years ago, prehistoric **reptiles** lived on Earth. Most scientists believe that these reptiles were the **ancestors** of birds.

Birds lay eggs, like reptiles, but they are **warm-blooded** animals, like **mammals**. Their body temperature stays about the same no matter what the temperature is around them.

Scales

Like reptiles, birds have scales on their legs and feet.

Flying feathers

Wing

Claws

Birds can be tiny, like hummingbirds, or huge, like an ostrich.

The ostrich is the biggest bird in the world. An adult male can be taller than the tallest pro basketball players!

AMAZING BIRD FACT

Ostriches are too heavy to fly, but they can run fast. Their top speed is about 45 miles (70 kilometers) per hour.

Bird Habitats

This robin built a nest on a shelf in a garden shed!

A **habitat** is the place where a plant or an animal lives. Birds live in warm places, such as rain forests, and cold places, such as Antarctica. Many birds live close to people, in cities or around farms.

Birds live in many habitats all over the world.

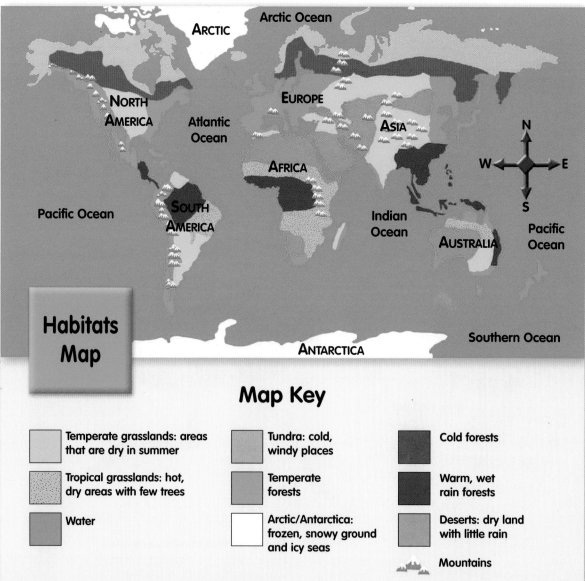

Habitats Map

Map Key

- **Temperate grasslands: areas that are dry in summer**
- **Tropical grasslands: hot, dry areas with few trees**
- **Water**
- **Tundra: cold, windy places**
- **Temperate forests**
- **Arctic/Antarctica: frozen, snowy ground and icy seas**
- **Cold forests**
- **Warm, wet rain forests**
- **Deserts: dry land with little rain**
- **Mountains**

Emperor penguins live in Antarctica, the coldest place on Earth.

Macaws live in warm rain forests.

Emperor penguins are the biggest type of penguin.

Water-loving birds live beside rivers, lakes, or the sea. Gulls and other seabirds build their nests on cliffs. They gather in big groups called colonies.

Like other seabirds, gannets gather in large nesting colonies.

Wings and Flying

Swifts catch insects in the air.

Birds have very light bodies. Their bones are hollow, or empty inside, but very strong. Birds have powerful muscles to beat their wings up and down. Flying uses up energy, so birds spend a lot of time eating.

You can tell how a bird flies from the shape of its wing. A swift has long, pointed wings for fast flying.

A buzzard has broad wings for gliding and soaring high in the sky.

Buzzards fly high, looking for mice and other food on the ground.

AMAZING BIRD FACT
A robin's short wings are good for short, quick flights in search of insects to eat.

The wingspan of the wandering albatross can be up to 12 feet (4 meters) across!

Wandering albatrosses are rarely seen on land.

The wandering albatross has the largest **wingspan** of all birds. It spends most of its life flying over the ocean. The albatross flies to land only when it is time to **mate**, lay eggs, and raise its young.

Many baby birds fly without being shown how. They tumble out of the nest, spread their wings, and fly. Other babies need to practice.

A baby albatross practices flapping its wings.

Mom Meets Dad

Most birds **breed** every year, usually in spring. Some birds stay together as a pair for life. Other birds have a new partner each year. Some females have chicks with more than one male in the same year.

Male and female swans pair for life.

Tail

Some male birds have colorful feathers that attract females. The male peacock shows off to the female, called a peahen, by spreading his tail feathers like a fan.

Many male birds sing to attract a female to their territory. They defend their territory and their female by chasing away other males.

Peacocks have the longest tail feathers of any bird.

Some pairs of birds dance together before they mate. Most often, the male dances for the female. He may also whistle or make other noises to get her attention.

As part of their dance, some male birds spread their wings and point their beaks into the air.

This female swan collects leaves to put in her nest.

Eggs and Nests

Many female birds make their own nest. Others get help from their partner. Some birds make the nest before they mate, and some do it afterward. The female lays her eggs in the nest.

Some birds make nests from grass, twigs, and leaves. The flamingo makes a nest of mud with a hollowed-out top.

The white stork's nest is made of sticks. The storks add more sticks every year, so the nest gets bigger and bigger!

The female flamingo lays one or two eggs at a time.

The female stork lays up to four eggs in her nest.

Adult woodpecker

Chick

This great spotted woodpecker makes its nest in a hole in a tree.

This bald eagle is sitting on her eggs.

Female birds sit on their eggs to keep them warm. This practice is called **incubation**. Some types of male birds help with this job, too. They also bring food for the female.

Chicks **hatch** from the eggs. Many chicks are helpless. Mom and dad bring food for them.

13

What Is a Life Cycle?

A **life cycle** is the different stages that an animal or a plant goes through in its life. This diagram shows the usual life cycle of a bird.

A robin chick eats about 140 bugs, spiders, and worms a day!

1

An adult male and female bird meet and mate.

THE
LIFE CYCLE OF
A ROBIN

6

5

Like the young robin shown here, the chicks leave the nest when they are ready to go off on their own. Some parents teach their chicks how to fly.

The parents bring the chicks their food.

Amazing Bird Life Cycles

Arctic tern

In the pages that follow, we will learn about the life cycles of some amazing birds—from the athletic Arctic tern to the tricky killdeer.

Killdeer

2

The female lays eggs in a nest.

Robins live in Europe, North Africa, and parts of Asia. American robins live in North America.

3

The female sits on the eggs to keep them warm. Some types of male birds bring the female food while she sits on the nest.

4

The eggs hatch. Many chicks are blind and have no feathers when they hatch.

Hornbill

Hornbills live in the forests of Africa and Asia. The hornbill uses its large beak, or bill, to eat fruit and catch insects, lizards, and snakes.

This southern ground hornbill feeds on the ground.

Most types of hornbills find their food in trees, but some feed on the ground.

The great Indian hornbill lives in trees.

LIFE CYCLE FACTS

The female hornbill lays up to six eggs at a time. The chicks hatch in 30 to 40 days.

Hornbills nest in holes in trees. The female lays her eggs and then shuts herself inside. She blocks the entrance with a wall made from droppings mixed with mud and squashed fruit.

A female hornbill takes a last look before she blocks the nest entrance.

The male hornbill passes the female food through a slit in the wall.

After the eggs hatch, the female stays in the hole for up to three months. As the chicks grow, the space gets too crowded. Then the mother breaks open the wall and climbs out. The chicks stay in the hole until they are ready to fly.

A male red-knobbed hornbill feeds his hidden mate.

A killdeer will run at a horse or cow to stop it from stepping on her eggs.

Killdeer

Killdeers live on grasslands. They eat worms, beetles, grasshoppers, and snails. Killdeers nest on the ground, where there are many dangers. The chicks can run as soon as they hatch!

Killdeer eggs have brown speckles that act as **camouflage**. This hides the eggs from **predators**.

Eggs

Killdeer chicks already have feathers when they hatch.

Chicks on the ground have nowhere to hide. They must sit very still in the grass.

The killdeer has a
trick to protect its family
from foxes and other predators.
The bird drags one of its wings on
the ground so it looks injured.

Thinking it will get an easy meal,
the fox follows the killdeer. The
killdeer leads the fox away from
the nest and then flies away. The
chicks keep very still and quiet
until their mother returns.

**LIFE CYCLE
FACTS**
The female killdeer
normally lays four eggs
at a time. The chicks
hatch after about
25 days.

Penguin pairs stay
together for years.

Emperor Penguin

Penguins cannot fly. They use their wings as flippers for swimming in the sea. Emperor penguins do not build nests. After mating, the female lays one egg. The male holds the egg on his feet to keep it warm.

The new chick stays warm on Dad's feet!

The female goes off to the sea to catch fish. Sometimes emperor penguins walk for 60 miles (100 km) to get to the sea.

LIFE CYCLE FACTS

The female emperor penguin lays one egg at a time. The chick hatches after about 65 days.

The male cares for the egg all winter. In spring, the egg hatches and the female returns from the sea with food for the chick.

After the egg hatches, the male and female take turns caring for the chick and going fishing.

The chicks cannot swim until they have grown adult feathers. After four or five months, their feathers have grown in, and they are able to go to the sea to find food on their own.

The parent penguin coughs up partly digested fish from its throat for the chick.

Arctic terns catch fish by plunging into the sea.

Arctic Tern

The Arctic tern is the champion bird traveler. Each year, this small seabird **migrates** from the Arctic to Antarctica and back again. Arctic terns fly about 20,000 miles (35,000 km) every year.

Arctic terns have two summers every year.

When it is winter in the northern part of the world, it is summer in the south. Arctic terns fly south to escape the cold northern winter. When the southern summer ends, the terns fly north again.

ARCTIC TERN MIGRATION ROUTE

Arctic

Atlantic Ocean   Africa

South America

Antarctica

Every year, the Arctic tern migrates from north to south and back again.

Arctic terns pair for life. They mate and lay their eggs in the Arctic.

Chick

The parent terns raise their chicks during the short Arctic summer. When it's time to fly south, the parents guide the youngsters to show them the way.

LIFE CYCLE FACTS

The female Arctic tern lays two or three eggs at a time. The chicks hatch after about 24 days.

The parents bring the chicks fish to eat.

The satin bowerbird has blue-black feathers and bright blue eyes.

Bowerbird

Bowerbirds live in Australia and New Guinea. The male builds a little archway, called a bower, to attract a mate. He puts colorful things, such as stones, feathers, and shells, inside the bower.

The male dances in and out of his bower. Females visit several bowers before deciding on a mate.

Bower

LIFE CYCLE FACTS

The female satin bowerbird lays two or three eggs at a time. The chicks hatch after 15 to 30 days.

Sometimes males steal decorations from each other's bowers!

This bird is stealing a blue block for its bower.

Satin bowerbirds like the color blue. A male may collect blue drinking straws, pieces of blue plastic, and even ballpoint pens!

Male

Female

The female bowerbird inspects a bower.

After mating, the female bowerbird makes a saucer-shaped nest for her eggs. The male doesn't help. He is more interested in his bower.

Tailorbirds don't mind being around humans. Some nest in people's backyards.

Tailorbird

The tailorbird lives in South Asia. It makes a very unusual nest! Just as a tailor sews cloth to make clothes, the tailorbird sews leaves together to make a nest.

The tailorbird chooses a long, wide leaf to become its nest. Using its beak as a needle, it sews the edges of the leaf together to make a bag shape.

Leaf

For thread, the bird uses plant fibers or a spiderweb. The bird makes neat, tight stitches. Inside the leaf bag, the bird makes a cozy nest from spiderwebs and other soft materials.

Soft nest material

Stitches

Leaf bag

The chicks have left this tailorbird nest. The unused leaf bag has dried out.

The female sits on the eggs to keep them warm before they hatch. Both parents feed insects and spiders to the chicks.

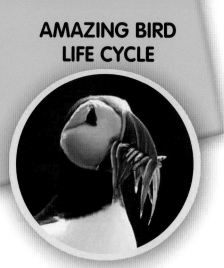

Puffins eat fish. They can carry 10 small fish sideways in their beaks.

Puffin

The puffin is a seabird that nests on cliffs. Puffins are great swimmers. Male and female puffins do a courtship dance in which they bob heads and touch beaks. They then mate out at sea.

Using their beaks and feet, the puffin mates dig a nest **burrow**. Some puffins nest inside empty rabbit holes.

LIFE CYCLE FACTS
The female puffin lays one egg at a time. The chick hatches after about 40 days.

A male and female do a courtship dance.

Burrow entrance

Inside the burrow, the female lays one egg. The parents take turns incubating the egg and catching fish for the chick when it hatches.

When the chick is six weeks old, the parents leave it. After a week on its own, the chick leaves the burrow.

Nest material

Puffin chick

The chick rushes to the sea, usually at night, when there are few rats, seagulls, and other predators around.

Swallows stick their nests to houses or cave walls, using their gummy spit as glue.

That's Amazing!

Every type of bird has a different way of caring for its chicks. Birds build nests in all sorts of places. They lay eggs of different sizes. Once their chicks hatch, parents have many ways to keep them well fed.

The cuckoo lays its egg in the nest of another bird and then leaves. The other bird does not notice the strange egg. The cuckoo chick hatches after 12 days and pushes the other bird's eggs or chicks out of the nest.

The cuckoo gets all the food and is soon bigger than its new parents!

Cuckoo chick

Wagtail adult

Nest

Ostrich egg

Chicken egg

African weaverbirds nest in colonies. Each pair of birds weaves a nest from grass and leaves.

Ostriches lay the biggest eggs of any bird. An ostrich egg is 24 times larger than a chicken egg. A hummingbird's egg is the smallest. It's about the size of a pea!

AMAZING BIRD FACT
Ostrich fathers care for their chicks. Mom doesn't help at all.

31

Glossary

ancestors: parents, grandparents, great-grandparents—all the individuals that came before

breed: to mate and have babies

burrow: an underground tunnel or hole where some animals live

camouflage: colors, marks, or a shape that hides an animal from predators and its prey

habitat: the natural conditions in which a plant or an animal lives

hatch: to break out of an egg

incubation: keeping eggs warm before they hatch

life cycle: the series of changes that an animal or a plant goes through in its life

mammals: warm-blooded animals that feed their babies milk

mate: to come together to make eggs or babies

migrates: travels a long way to find food or a place to breed

predators: animals that hunt and kill other animals for food

reptiles: animals that are covered in scales. Snakes, lizards, and crocodiles are reptiles.

warm-blooded: describes an animal whose body temperature stays the same no matter how hot or cold the air or water is around it

wingspan: the distance from the tip of one wing to the tip of the other

Index